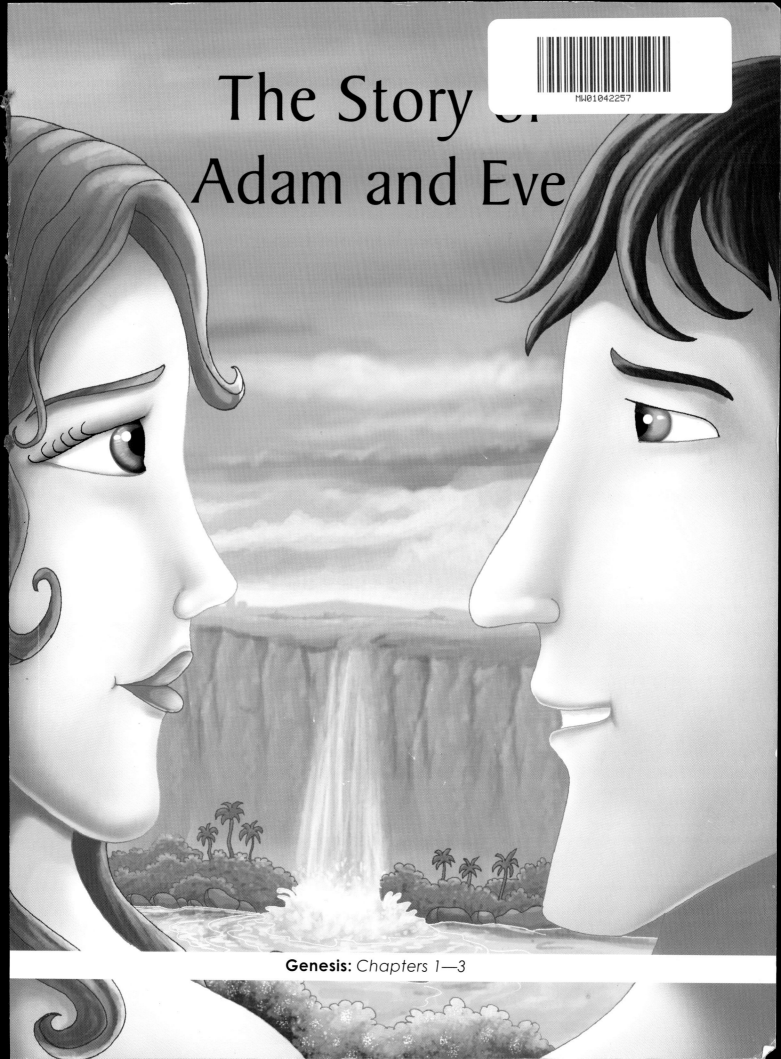

The Story of Adam and Eve

Genesis: *Chapters 1—3*

Our Earth is very old. No one knows when it was created. But long before the Earth or the sun or the stars existed, God was there. He always was. God commanded and the Earth and the heavens came into being. The Earth was a great smoking ball, with land and water mingled in one mass. There was darkness all around as there was no light. And there was no life upon the Earth.

Seeing the darkness upon the Earth, God said, 'Let there be light!' And then, light began to dawn upon the Earth. Half of the time there was light and half of the time there was darkness, just as it is now. God called the dark time *night*, and the time with light, *day*. All this was done by God on the *first* day.

On the *second* day, at God's command, the dark clouds all around the Earth began to break and the sky was visible. The water that was in the clouds began to separate from the water that was on the Earth. God called the sky that stretched on the Earth—Heaven.

On the *third* day God said, 'Let the water on the Earth come together in one place and let the dry land rise up.' And so it was. God called the great body of water, *sea*, and the dry land, *Earth*. When He was satisfied, He said, 'Let grass, trees, flowers and fruits grow on the Earth.' And at once the Earth began to be green and bright with grass, flowers and trees bearing fruit.

On the *fourth* day God said, 'Let the sun, the moon and the stars be visible from the Earth.' And so it was! The sun began to shine during the day, and the moon and the stars began to shine at night.

On the *fifth* day God said, 'Let there be fishes in the sea, and let there be birds to fly in the air.' So different types of fish—big and small—began to swim in the sea. And the birds began to fly in the air just as they do now.

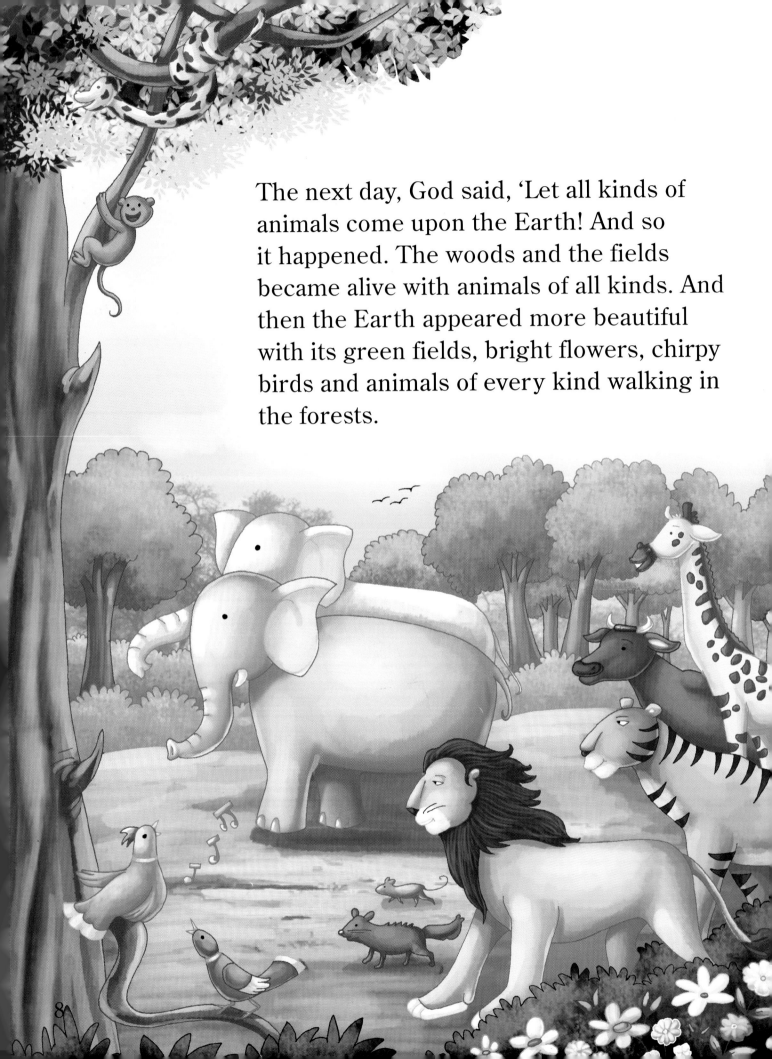

The next day, God said, 'Let all kinds of animals come upon the Earth! And so it happened. The woods and the fields became alive with animals of all kinds. And then the Earth appeared more beautiful with its green fields, bright flowers, chirpy birds and animals of every kind walking in the forests.

But there were no people on the Earth. And so God said, 'I will make man who will be different from all other animals. He shall have a soul and shall be like Me!'
So God took some of the dust from the ground, and out of it he made a man. He breathed life into him and the man came alive! God named him Adam.

9

And then, so that the man might have a home, God made a beautiful garden on the Earth at a place where four rivers met. In this garden, trees grew and flowers bloomed. This was called *The Garden of Eden*. God gave this garden to Adam and told him to care for it and to live on the fruits that grew there.

But Adam was all alone in this beautiful garden. So God said, 'I will make a companion for Adam.' When Adam was asleep, God took a rib from Adam's side and made it into a woman. When God brought her to Adam, Adam called her Eve. Adam and Eve loved each other and lived happily in the beautiful garden.

So, in six days God created the Heaven, the Earth, the sea, and all that is in them. On the *seventh* day God rested. For quite some time, Adam and Eve lived in their beautiful garden. They did just as God told them to do, and did not know anything evil. One day God said to Adam and Eve, 'You may eat fruits of all the trees in the garden except one. In the middle of the garden grows a tree. You must never eat its fruit or you will die!'

Now among the animals that lived in the garden was a snake. One day, this snake asked Eve, 'Has God forbidden you to eat the fruit of any tree?'

'We can eat the fruit of all the trees except the one that stands in the middle of the garden. If we eat the fruit of that tree, God said that we will die,' answered Eve.

Hearing this, the snake replied, 'You will surely not die. But God knows that if you eat the fruit of that tree, you will become as wise as God for you will know what is good and what is evil!' So Eve took the fruit and ate it. And then, she gave some to Adam, which he ate too. Adam and Eve knew that they had disobeyed God. And so they hid when God called them. 'Why are you afraid to meet me? Have you eaten the forbidden fruit?' At this Adam said, 'Eve gave it to me and I ate it.'

God was furious at this. He said to Eve, 'What have you done?' When Eve told him about the snake and his advice, God angrily cursed the snake that it would crawl in the dust forever. He also cursed Adam and Eve saying that they would have to work hard and suffer all their lives.

After this, Adam and Eve were sent out of the Garden of Eden forever.